Getting to Know

SEA TURTLES

With the Sea Turtle Experts

J.P. TAYLOR

Getting to Know Sea Turtles
By J. P. Taylor
© Copyright 2022 John Paul Taylor Jr.
ISBN: 9798797043072 (Paperback)

Sea turtles are amazing animals! They live in the warmer waters of the oceans all around the world. In this book you will learn about the different kinds of sea turtles.

You will also meet some real sea turtle scientists. They will share interesting facts about sea turtles with you. So, are you ready? Just turn the page and let's get started!

Meet the Sea Turtle Scientists

Dr. Justin Perrault is the Director of Research at Loggerhead Marinelife Center. He has worked with sea turtles in the field and in the laboratory since 2006 and currently resides in West Palm Beach, Florida. Contact: jperrault@marinelife.org

Dr. Stephanie Köhnk has worked with sea turtles since 2007 in Costa Rica, Cape Verde and the Indian Ocean. She is currently coordinating the research projects for the Olive Ridley Project with a focus on population ecology, biogeography, reproductive biology and threats to sea turtles. Contact: info@oliveridleyproject.org

Dennis Klemm is the Sea Turtle Recovery Coordinator for the National Marine Fisheries Service's (NMFS) Southeast Region. He has been working at NMFS to conserve and recover sea turtle populations under the Endangered Species Act for 20 years. Contact: dennis.klemm@noaa.gov

Terry Norton, DVM, Diplomate ACZM, is the Director of Veterinary Services and Wildlife Health at the Georgia Sea Turtle Center and Jekyll Island Authority. He also provides veterinary care for the Turtle Hospital in Marathon, Florida, and St. Catherines Island Foundation wildlife programs. Contact: tnorton@jekyllisland.com

Dr. Daniel Evans is a Senior Research Biologist with the Sea Turtle Conservancy. He has worked in sea turtle conservation and research since 1996, with a focus on tracking sea turtle migration and habitat use using satellites. Dan also manages the Florida Sea Turtle License Plate Grants Program. Contact: drevans@conserveturtles.org

In all the world there are only **7 kinds** of sea turtles. Their names are: loggerhead, leatherback, green, hawksbill, Kemp's ridley, olive ridley, and flatback. In this book you will learn about all of them.

All turtles are **reptiles**. A reptile is an animal with a backbone and skin that's covered with scales or plates. Reptiles are **cold-blooded**. That means their body temperature changes with the outside temperature. Most reptiles lay eggs with soft shells. Reptiles also **breathe air**.

But sea turtles live in the sea. How do they breathe?

Even though they live in the ocean, sea turtles breathe air like we do. They come up to the surface and get air with their nose. But, they can **hold their breath** for a very long time. If they are sleeping, they can hold their breath for several hours!

Sea turtles are different from most other turtles. Since they live in the ocean, they have **flippers** for swimming instead of legs and feet for walking.

Like us, sea turtles have to drink fresh water. But the water of the ocean is very salty. So sea turtles have special pockets in their heads called **salt glands** that help them get rid of the salt in the water.

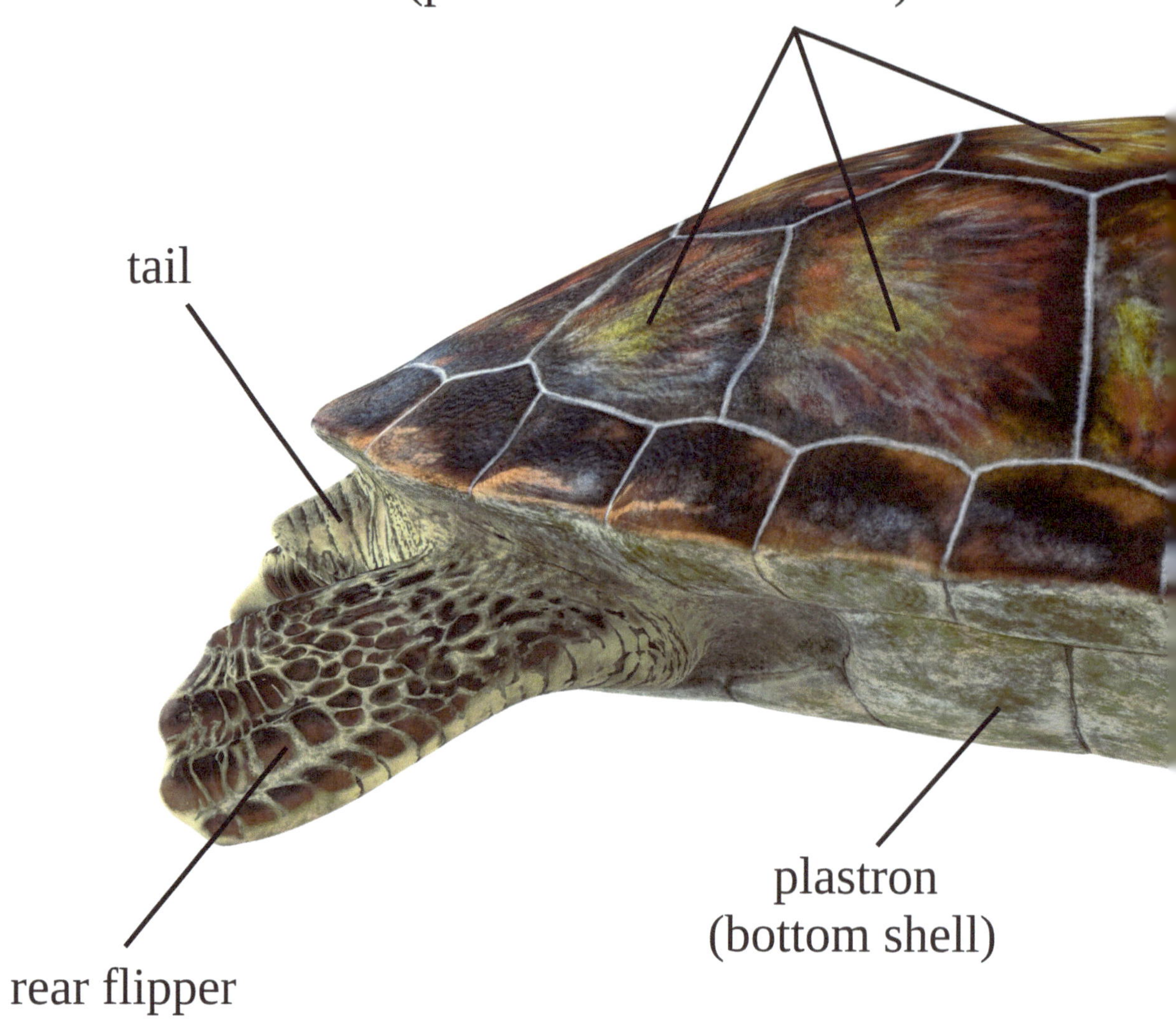

scutes
(plates of a turtle's shell)
tail
rear flipper
plastron
(bottom shell)

carapace
(top shell)
eye
nose
claw
front flipper

The temperature inside a sea turtle nest determines if the hatchlings will be male or female. Cooler nests have more male hatchlings. Warmer nests have more females.

Most sea turtles come on shore **during the night** to lay their eggs. They crawl on the beach and dig their nest in the sand. The nests they dig look like an upside down **light bulb**.

When the mother sea turtle finishes laying her eggs, she covers the nest with sand. Then she crawls back across the beach and into the sea.

Sea turtle eggs look like ping-pong balls. The **shells are soft**, not hard like a chicken egg.

The **females** (mother turtles) are careful to dig their nests above the **high tide** line (so water from the ocean will not reach them). If water gets into the nest the babies in the eggs could drown. Most sea turtle eggs hatch around 60 days after being laid.

Sea turtle **hatchlings** (babies) have a special part to their upper jaw called a **caruncle**. They use it to break out of their eggs. The caruncle is like a temporary tooth. The caruncle falls off after they have used it.

Once they are out of their eggs, the hatchlings wait together in the nest. When the time is right, usually **at night**, they all work together to climb out.

The hatchlings head for the **natural light** of the ocean. But other lights around the beach (like street lights, parking lots, homes, and cars) may make them crawl the wrong way.

They must crawl as quickly as possible to avoid **predators** (animals who would eat them), like birds and crabs.

Once they reach the ocean, some sea turtles swim to an area called the **Sargasso Sea**. This is an area where there are large mats of seaweed that float on the surface of the ocean. It gives sea turtles and other young animals a good place to live while they are growing up.

As hatchlings leave the nest and head to the water, things on the beach can trap or block them. So remember to fill-in any holes you dig, knock your sand castles down, and pick up anything you brought before you leave. A sea turtle's life could depend on it!

Sargassum gives turtles a safe place to hide from predators and food to eat, like barnacles, crab larvae, and fish larvae. When they get older, sea turtles return to areas closer to shore.

The large mats of brown seaweed are called **sargassum**. Sargassum is a kind of algae. It has leaves and branches. It also has berries that help it float in the water.

The **leatherback** is the **largest** of all the sea turtles. They live in the Atlantic, Pacific, and Indian Oceans around the world.

Leatherbacks do not have scales on their shells. They have thick, black **skin** that stretches over the bones of their shell. The shell has **ridges** that go from the front to the back. Leatherback sea turtles have really big front **flippers**. Their back flippers are shaped like paddles. They do not have claws on their flippers.

Leatherbacks eat mostly **jellyfish**. Since plastic bags look a lot like jellyfish, leatherbacks sometimes eat them and can get very sick or even die.

Leatherback sea turtles are **great swimmers**. They are found in more places than any other reptile on the planet.

Adult leatherbacks can grow to be 5 to 6 feet long. They can weigh over 1,000 pounds. Leatherback sea turtles can live to be over 40 years old.

Leatherbacks are amazing animals. They can dive deeper than a nuclear submarine! They have leathery skin, not a hard shell, so their shell can compress, and not crack, when they dive.

Sea turtles can be curious and can have a bit of a personality. Green turtles tend to be fairly mellow.

Green sea turtles live in the warmer parts of the ocean around the world. They nest in over 80 countries. Green sea turtles are the largest of all the **hard-shelled** sea turtles. The leatherback is much bigger, but does not have a hard shell.

Can you guess why they are called green sea turtles? It's not because they are green on the outside. Their inside fat layers are green! Why? Adult green sea turtles are **herbivores** (eat plants), and they especially love sea grasses. There is even a type of sea grass called **turtle grass**.

The female turtles lay around **110 to 120 eggs** in each nest. The eggs hatch about 60 days later. Like loggerheads, baby green sea turtles swim to the **Sargasso Sea** to spend their early years.

Adults grow to be 3 to 4 feet long. They weigh between 250 and 400 pounds.

Like green sea turtles, **Loggerheads** live in the warmer areas of the Atlantic, Pacific, and Indian oceans around the world. They also live in the Mediterranean Sea.

They get their name from their **large head** and strong **jaws**. These powerful jaws allow them to eat **shellfish** (like crabs, whelks, and conchs) by crushing their shells. The top of a loggerhead's shell is a reddish-brown color.

Adult female loggerheads lay **about 100 eggs** in each nest. They often nest 3 to 5 times a season. After about 2 months the hatchlings crawl out of the nest and to the water. Sometimes **predators** (like fire ants, crabs, raccoons, and dogs) can eat the babies.

Adults usually grow to be between 2 ½ to 3 ½ feet long. Loggerheads weigh about 200 to more than 350 pounds.

Loggerhead turtles can lay more than 3-5 nests in a season. We actually had a loggerhead tie the world record for the most number of nests laid with 8, but 6 is our average number of nests.

Hawksbill sea turtles spend most of their time around coral reefs. They help keep the coral reefs healthy by feeding on sponges to keep their populations in balance.

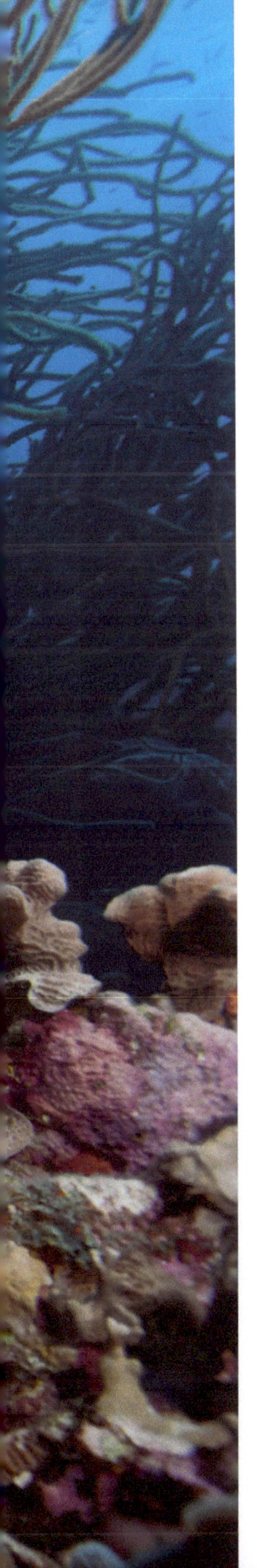

Hawksbill sea turtles live in **tropical** (warmer) waters around the world. They are named for the way their heads look. They have a mouth that looks like the beak of a hawk. This lets them get into places where they find their food.

Their favorite food is **sea sponges**! These sponges live in coral reefs like those you see in the photo. Hawksbills will also eat other small animals including squid, shrimp, and jellyfish.

They are famous for their beautiful shells. The shell is more rounded in the front and comes to a point in the back. Sadly, in some places people still make and sell jewelry made from hawksbill shells. This is one of the reasons hawksbills are so endangered.

Hawksbill sea turtles lay an average of **130 to 160 eggs**. They grow to be 2 to 3 feet long and weigh between 100 and 150 pounds.

The **Kemp's ridley** is the smallest of all the sea turtles. They are also the **most endangered** of all sea turtles.

Adult Kemp's ridleys live in the shallow waters along the coast of the Gulf of Mexico. Younger Kemp's ridleys travel along the coast of the United States from Florida all the way to New England.

Kemp's ridley sea turtles have **strong jaws**. This helps them crush and eat their favorite foods like shrimp, crabs, and clams. They also eat fish and jellyfish.

Kemp's ridleys and olive ridleys are the only 2 **species** (kinds) of sea turtles that nest in what scientists call an "**arribada**." This is when hundreds of female turtles come on shore to nest all at the same time.

Each nest contains about **100 eggs**. After 50 to 60 days the eggs hatch and the hatchlings all scramble toward the sea.

Adult Kemp's ridleys grow to be about 2 feet long. They weigh between 70 and 100 pounds.

Most sea turtles nest on many beaches across many countries, but Kemp's ridley turtles do almost all of their nesting on a stretch of beaches from central Mexico to southwest Texas, along the western Gulf of Mexico.

The biggest olive ridley arribadas are along the coast of India, and the Pacific coast of Costa Rica. Kemp's ridley arribadas only happen in a very small area on the coast of the Gulf of Mexico.

The **olive ridley** is the second smallest of all the sea turtles. They live in the warmer parts of the Atlantic, Pacific, and Indian Oceans around the world.

Olive ridleys have a heart-shaped shell. Hatchlings are charcoal gray. Adults' shells are a darker **olive green color**. That is how they got their name. Each of their flippers may have **one or two claws**.

Olive ridleys are **omnivores** (eat animals and plants). They eat algae as well as lobsters, shrimps, crabs, fish, and jellyfish.

Like Kemp's ridleys, olive ridley sea turtles often nest in what scientists call an **arribada**. This is when hundreds of female turtles come on shore to nest all at the same time.

Their nests usually contain about **100 eggs**. After 50 to 60 days the eggs hatch and the hatchlings all head toward the sea together.

Adult olive ridleys grow to be 2 to 2 ½ feet long. They weigh between 75 and 100 pounds.

Olive ridley turtles spend most of their life in the open ocean far away from land. During their time at sea, they can dive over 200 meters (more than 500 feet) deep.

B
A
C
D
AUSTRALIA

Can you tell how the **flatback** sea turtle got its name? Of course! It's because its shell is so flat compared to all the other sea turtles. The shell is smooth looking and curves up at the edges.

Flatback sea turtles do not swim all over the ocean. As you can see on the map, they stay in the waters around **Australia**.

Flatback sea turtles **lay about 50 eggs** in their nests. That's about half as many as the other sea turtles, but the eggs and hatchlings are bigger than most of the others. Sometimes saltwater crocodiles attack the females as they are nesting on the beach.

What do they eat? Flatbacks are **omnivores**, that means they eat both animals and plants. They feed mostly on animals like shrimp, crabs, soft corals and jellyfish, but sometimes will eat seaweed too.

Adult flatbacks can weigh up to 200 pounds or more and are about 3 feet long. Scientists believe they can live to be 50 to 100 years old.

The DANGERS of Being a Sea Turtle

Fishing Gear (like lines, hooks, and nets) can trap and injure or kill sea turtles. The turtles are often caught in nets and pulled aboard ships. **Ghost gear** (long fishing lines and nets that have been cut or let go by fishing boats) is a big problem in many areas of the ocean.

Boats are a big danger for sea turtles. Many turtles live near the shore where lots of boats come and go. They must come up to breathe and sometimes relax just floating at the surface of the water, where they can be hit and injured by boats.

Predators (like crabs, raccoons, foxes and even dogs and fire ants) will get into sea turtle nests and eat the eggs. Hatchlings on the beach may be attacked by birds. When they reach the ocean hatchlings may be eaten by fish and other predators in the water.

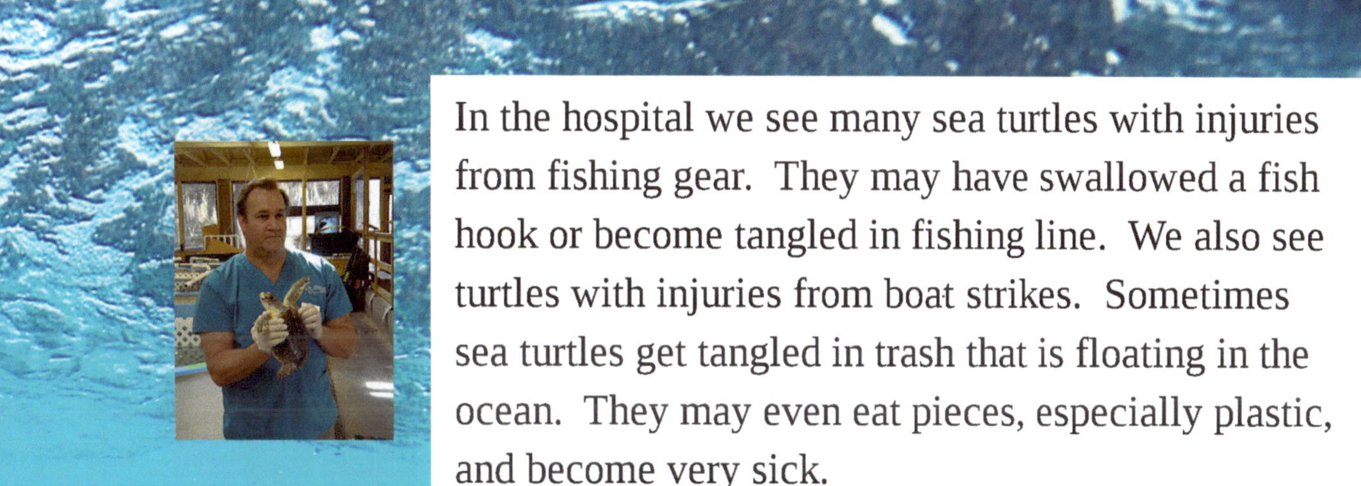

In the hospital we see many sea turtles with injuries from fishing gear. They may have swallowed a fish hook or become tangled in fishing line. We also see turtles with injuries from boat strikes. Sometimes sea turtles get tangled in trash that is floating in the ocean. They may even eat pieces, especially plastic, and become very sick.

Building Construction

Many beaches where sea turtles used to nest now have big buildings on them. This can cause the nesting females to become confused and even lost. Sea turtles have even been seen falling into swimming pools.

Lights around nesting beaches can be very bad for sea turtles. Hatchlings normally head to the sea going towards the lighter horizon of the ocean. Lights in parking lots and buildings, and even headlights and flashlights, can lead them in the wrong direction.

REFERENCES

NOAA Fisheries – fisheries.noaa.gov

Sea Turtle Conservancy – conserveturtles.org

Loggerhead Marinelife Center – marinelife.org

Olive Ridley Projecct – oliveridleyproject.org

Georgia Sea Turtle Center – gstc.jekyllisland.com

SWOT – seaturtlestatus.org

See Turtles – seeturtles.org

Oceana – oceana.org

University of Central Florida – ucf.edu

www.ingramcontent.com/pod-product-compliance
Lightning Source LLC
Chambersburg PA
CBHW042111110726
48006CB00002B/597